CHICAGO
THE CITY AT A GLANCE

North Avenue Beach
Chicagoans head here in the steamy summer to congregate at North Avenue Beach House (1603 N Lake Shore Drive, T 312 742 7529), a massive beached ocean liner where you can eat and rent bikes and chairs.

Lake Point Tower
Forty years on, Lake Point Tower is still one of the city's choicest addresses, thanks to fantastic views of the lake and a private park.
Navy Pier Park

John Hancock Center
Dark, brooding, dangerous-looking and one of the most charismatic skyscrapers in the world, the John Hancock Center signposts the start of the city's glittering Magnificent Mile.
See p009

Aon Center
Formerly the Standard Oil Building, this strict, severe and rather lovely tower looms in the background of shots of Millennium Park.
See p011

Lincoln Park
This is Chicago's Central Park – six miles of lush greenery and sports facilities, with a lakefront path perfect for running and cycling.

Marina City
Bertrand Goldberg's Marina City buildings are growing into their looks, and are charming concrete emblems of 1960s idealism.
See p015

Sears Tower
The tallest building in the States, actually nine bundled towers, is still one of the world's most elegant mega-structures.
See p013

INTRODUCTION
THE CHANGING FACE OF THE URBAN SCENE

You know when a city is in the ascendant and when it is in decline. You can see it and feel it. And Chicago is definitely in the ascendant. It has been a long time coming, but the 'city of broad shoulders', a place that's associated with organised crime, political cynicism, sink estates, architecture at its most daring, and music, Chicago jazz and blues, that might be the truest of American art forms, is once again a confident, ambitious, hopeful place.

Chicago is the most American of America's metropolises, and it has paid for it. Once an economic rival to New York, it suffered in comparison to Gotham the global city, then felt the pain as the sun and glitter of LA superseded its meat and smoke. Now Chicago, important and interesting because it is not LA or NYC, is on the up. It's true that The Loop, the city's traditional heart, remains an odd proposition. Look skywards and you'll see glittering corporate towers and the iconography of civic ambition. At street level, though, there are shabby storefronts and, often, the shuffling poor. But right there is <u>Millennium Park</u> (see p009), a new public space of radical ambition. The Magnificent Mile is glitzier than ever, and around this, in Bucktown and Wicker Park, regeneration is obvious. As even the notorious Cabrini Green is advanced upon by the forces of betterment, you know this is a city being remade. Perhaps that is the appeal. Chicago is still working out how it gets from what it was to what it wants to be. And that is truly invigorating.

ESSENTIAL INFO
FACTS, FIGURES AND USEFUL ADDRESSES

TOURIST OFFICE
Chicago Office of Tourism
78 E Washington Street
T 312 744 2400
www.cityofchicago.org

TRANSPORT
Car hire
Avis
O'Hare International Airport
T 773 825 4600
www.avis.com
Hertz
3151 N Halsted Street
T 773 832 1912
www.hertz.com
CTA
Chicago Transit Authority
T 312 836 7000
www.transitchicago.com
Taxis
Chicago Carriage Cab Co
T 312 326 2221
www.chicagocarriagecab.com
Yellow Cab Chicago
T 312 225 7440
www.yellowcabchicago.com

EMERGENCY SERVICES
Ambulance/Fire/Police
T 911
24-hour pharmacy
Walgreens
641 N Clark Street
T 312 587 1416
www.walgreens.com

CONSULATE
British Consulate-General
400 N Michigan Avenue
T 312 970 3800
www.britainusa.com/chicago

MONEY
American Express
Suite 105, 605 N Michigan Avenue
T 312 943 7840
travel.americanexpress.com

POSTAL SERVICES
Post Office
2522 W Lawrence Avenue
T 773 561 8633
Shipping
UPS
T 312 372 2727

BOOKS
The Adventures of Augie March
by Saul Bellow (Penguin Classics)
Masterpieces of Chicago Architecture by
John Zukowsky and Martha Thorne (Rizzoli)
The Devil in the White City
by Erik Larson (Bantam)

WEBSITES
Architecture
www.architecture.org
Magazine
www.chicagoist.com
Newspaper
www.chicagotribune.com

COST OF LIVING
**Taxi from O'Hare International Airport
to city centre**
£22
Cappuccino
£1.30
Packet of cigarettes
£3.80
Daily newspaper
£0.25
Bottle of champagne
£45

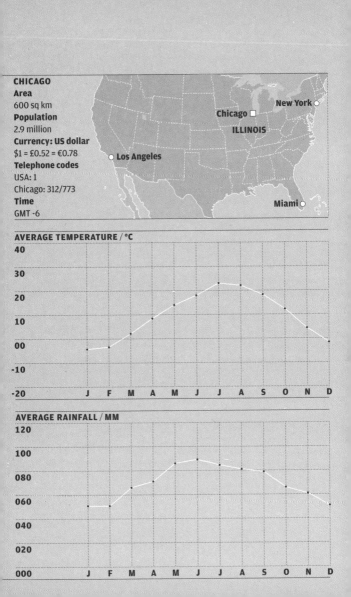

CHICAGO
Area
600 sq km
Population
2.9 million
Currency: US dollar
$1 = £0.52 = €0.78
Telephone codes
USA: 1
Chicago: 312/773
Time
GMT -6

New York
Chicago
ILLINOIS
Los Angeles
Miami

AVERAGE TEMPERATURE / °C

40
30
20
10
00
-10
-20
J F M A M J J A S O N D

AVERAGE RAINFALL / MM

120
100
080
060
040
020
000
J F M A M J J A S O N D

NEIGHBOURHOODS
THE AREAS YOU NEED TO KNOW AND WHY

To help you navigate the city, we've chosen the most interesting districts (see below and the map inside the back cover) and colour-coded our featured venues, according to their location; those venues that are outside these areas are not coloured.

THE LOOP

This is the city's centre and the heart of the architects' playground – innumerable skyscrapers cluster in between Millennium Park to the east and the financial district and river to the west. The L train clunks around it, two storeys up, providing the best viewing platform, while at ground level drab chain stores abound.

LINCOLN PARK

For the last 30 years, this comfortable residential zone, named after Chicago's largest park, has been inhabited by the city's young monied folk. West Armitage offers a concentration of once-cool retail and eating opportunities, now put in the shade by Wicker Park and the West Loop.

SOUTH LOOP

After decades in the doldrums, the South Loop is looking up, with loft conversions and trendy eateries bringing in a young crowd. Many streets are still lined by the looming warehouses that formed the backdrop to Al Capone's misdemeanours, which adds somehow to the charm.

NEAR NORTH

Bisected by the Magnificent Mile, a stretch of Michigan Avenue lined with uptown shopping and high-end hotels, this is often where visitors first land. Some of the city's most distinctive landmarks are here too. River North is home to an established art community, their galleries and haunts.

WEST LOOP

The meatpacking district and its surrounds make up the West Loop. Early regenerators included Harpo Studios (Oprah's base) and Hoops basketball gym (see p094). Now the former warehouses are being colonised by galleries, loft dwellers and fashionable restaurants and shops, most preserving the area's industrial roots in their design.

GOLD COAST

Named after the colour of the money in its residents' coffers, this is where you'll find some of Chicago's most extravagant mansions, concentrated around Astor Street. Oak Street Beach provides locals with a sandy playground, Oak Street with Fifth Avenue shopping opportunities.

LAKE VIEW

Though it adjoins the lake, not much of this area offers views of it. Largely residential, it absorbs a number of smaller 'hoods such as Wrigleyville, which grew up around the 1914 stadium (see p089), and Boystown, the hub of Chicago's gay community, around the Halsted and Clark intersection.

WICKER PARK

This is the home ground of the music and art crowd. It's a cosy, laid-back and largely low-rise district, which offers the city's tightest conglomeration of independent clothes, interior and food boutiques, cool neighbourhood restaurants and cafés, and some of its prettiest townhouses.

LANDMARKS

THE SHAPE OF THE CITY SKYLINE

No other modern city has attempted to create as many landmark structures as Chicago. A collective and corporate will – as well as a certain civic chippiness – has seen America's then second, now third, city send up the first skyscrapers and spend the next century sending them ever higher while refining and redefining the form.

It makes for a skyline, rising out of the massive flatness of the Midwest and Great Lakes, which is not only uniquely striking – it's not as dense as New York's but there's an unmatched historical and stylistic stretch – but also makes knowing where you are in the city pretty simple. The two dark giants, the Sears Tower (see p013) and the John Hancock Center (see p057), bookend the downtown area. Meanwhile, at street level, a passion for public art means that every landmark building must have an accompanying grand sculptural statement and Chicago is dotted with pieces by Chagall, Picasso, Dubuffet, Oldenburg and Calder.

No surprise then that the latest city landmark is a collection of monumental public, and truly public, art. Millennium Park (see p058) might have missed the end-of-century party by four years, but its Crown Fountain by Jaume Plensa, Cloud Gate by Anish Kapoor, and the Jay Pritzker auditorium by Frank Gehry have become instant icons of a Chicago that is re-establishing itself as a great American city. Perhaps *the* great American city.
For full addresses, see Resources.

Skybridge

In 2003, this 39-storey apartment complex announced, in grand fashion, that there was something happening west of The Loop. The idea was simple: a skyscraper of loft-style apartments with high ceilings, open-plan living areas, lots of natural light and balconies. It works beautifully, because of the careful way in which the structure has been cut away in order to create 'neighbourhoods' within the building. The architect, Ralph Johnson, is the leading design partner at Perkins + Will, and is one of the most influential architects working in Chicago today; he is also responsible for the hugely successful Boeing HQ (100 N Riverside Plaza). His subsequent small residential tower, The Contemporaine (516 N Wells Street), recalls the big ideas of Skybridge.
1 N Halsted Street

Aon Center

Originally known as the Standard Oil Building and nicknamed 'Big Stan', this skyscraper reigned as Chicago's tallest building for just a year after its completion in 1972 (a helicopter had indicated its height at the groundbreaking ceremony). It was overtaken, and then some, by the Sears Tower (see p013). But the plum position and elegance of its design, by Edward Durell Stone, make it one of the city's most emblematic, if not best-loved, towers. The structure was clad in 43,000 marble panels, but when they started to come away in the 1980s they were replaced with white granite at a cost of £45m. The sculptural accompaniment, a series of metal wind rods, is by Harry Bertoia.

200 E Randolph Street

Lake Shore Drive apartments

Mies van der Rohe's relocation from Nazi Germany to Chicago was fortuitous in many ways. One stroke of luck was meeting the local developer Herbert Greenwald. Despite Greenwald's youth – he was 29 when they first collaborated in 1946 – he was brave enough to back Mies' vision (though apparently less generous when it came to prompt payments). And that vision found almost perfect expression in the four glass towers they put up between 1952 and 1956. The first two, at 860-880 Lake Shore Drive (above), were Mies' first to use glass and steel curtain walls with no interior load-bearing walls. The second pair, at 900-910 Lake Shore Drive, are a slightly darker echo of the first two towers. Chicagoans took to the buildings' light and height as if it were their birthright.
860-880 and 900-910 N Lake Shore Drive

Sears Tower

Completed in 1973, the 110-storey Sears Tower held the title of the world's tallest building until 1998. The nine bundled towers of different heights, by architect Bruce Graham of Skidmore, Owings & Merrill and engineer Fazlur Kahn, are wonderfully elegant. The cluster design (the idea allegedly came to Graham while he was considering the profile of cigarettes popping out of a pack) allows the building to soar, but also makes for a startling series of surges and setbacks. Sears Tower may have been overtaken by the Petronas Twin Towers in Kuala Lumpur, then the Taipei 101, but in terms of sheer architectural bravado, it stands alone among the world's super-tall buildings. *223 S Wacker Drive*

Tribune Tower

In 1922, Colonel Robert McCormick, the publisher of *The Chicago Tribune*, launched a contest to design the company's new HQ, and the entries heralded a new age in US architecture. The second place entry, by Finn Eliel Saarinen, was a muscular tower with Gothic flourishes that looked eerily like a truncated Empire State Building (a design by Walter Gropius and Adolf Meyer seems an even more startling premonition of Chicago to come). McCormick was no radical though and the winner was an outsized Gothic fantasy from New York firm Hood & Howells. The tower is topped by an almost absurd abstraction of Rouen Cathedral, flying buttresses and all. Now that Chicago boasts more modernism than it knows what to do with, the building is a welcome grand extravagance.

435 N Michigan Avenue

Marina City

Built in 1964 in an attempt to revitalise Chicago's then struggling city centre, the 'corn cob' towers are about as charming as 61-storey reinforced concrete towers can be charming — and in a city so rich in iconic buildings, stand right up there as totemic mascots (favourite local sons, the band Wilco, put Marina City on the cover of their 2002 album *Yankee Hotel Foxtrot*). The towers were designed by Bertrand Goldberg, who had studied under Mies van der Rohe at the Bauhaus, but after moving to Chicago in the 1930s developed a very non-Miesian sense of playfulness and a distaste for right angles. The arrival of Mies' IBM Building (330 N Wabash Avenue) in 1973 as Marina City's neighbour makes it clear just how much Goldberg had gone his own merry way. *300 N State Street*

HOTELS

WHERE TO STAY AND WHICH ROOMS TO BOOK

Chicago's hotel scene is highly evolved at the luxury end. There is an embarrassment of choice when it comes to deluxe suites, from the offerings of the Four Seasons (see p020) and The Ritz-Carlton (160 E Pearson Street, T 312 266 1000) to The Peninsula (see p022), consistently voted the finest hotel in the country. Other high-end staples are the Park Hyatt (800 N Michigan Avenue, T 312 335 1234) and a new Sofitel (20 E Chestnut Street, T 312 324 4000). Hotel refurbishments are frequent in this city, and what can be tired one year might have had a billion-dollar makeover the next.

For a city in love with modern architecture, hotel design here is, on the whole, surprisingly pedestrian, although there are one or two that come with added architectural interest, such as Hotel Burnham (1 W Washington Street, T 312 782 1111), a fine example of late 19th-century glass-and-steel skyscraping by Daniel Burnham, and the InterContinental (505 N Michigan Avenue, T 312 944 4100), a 1929 art deco building with a Romanesque swimming pool.

Where the city's hospitality industry flounders is at the boutique end of the market – hotels in the mould of New York's Maritime or Hudson are lacking. The James (see p018) is pretty much alone in this category, but Soho House is on its way to boost the field, and every 'for sale' sign on the meatpacking area's empty warehouses looks like an invitation to hotel entrepreneurs to join in.

For full addresses and room rates, see Resources.

W Chicago City Center

Housed in a stunning Beaux Arts building, which began life in 1929 as a handsome private members' club, the W City Center boasts a spectacular setting. But that's possibly all it can boast too much about. The building was converted in 2001 and the two-storey marble lobby (top storey, above), with its arched gallery and gold-leaf ceilings, has become The Living Room Bar with sofas, shiny cushions, projections and house music, making it feel like a half-empty nightclub. The 390 rooms are small but comfortable in that W way. The in-house Ristorante We serves up Tuscan cuisine, while the Whiskey Blue bar is busy, buzzy and hormone-charged. *172 W Adams Street, T 312 332 1200, www.whotels.com*

The James
This discreet and stylish hotel attracts
a design-conscious crowd. NYC architect
Deborah Berke (see p098) is responsible
for the earthy tones in the rooms, lofts
and apartments, such as the Loft Suite
(pictured). Chef David Burke has hit his
stride in the restaurant Primehouse, and
the J Bar attracts hip cocktail-suppers.
55 E Ontario Street, T 312 337 1000,
www.jameshotels.com

Four Seasons

As the rooms start on the 30th floor of The 900 Shops (T 312 915 3916) on N Michigan Avenue, a super-tony vertical mall, this hotel offers fantastic views and has an air of in-the-know clubbiness. A stately pile in the sky, it includes a large marble lobby with waterfall, a cigar bar and a restaurant. Elegant as it was, this floating palace was starting to look a little dark and dated, but a skilfully handled £16m refurb – there's a delicate touch of the David Collinses about the deco/moderne revamp – is brightening up the place and its 172 rooms and 163 suites, such as the Deluxe Executive Suite (above). We like the two-bedroom Author Suite on the 46th floor, which includes signed works by previous guests, Margaret Thatcher and Stephen King included.
120 E Delaware Place, T 312 280 8800, www.fourseasons.com

W Chicago Lakeshore

The consensus is that of the two Chicago Ws, the Lakeshore, overlooking Lake Michigan, is the better option, although it lacks the architectural drama of the City Center (see p017). Converted from a 1960s-built Days Inn, the Lakeshore aims for an even greater boutique feel and a fun-fun-fun factor. But the rooms and suites are in good, if over-designed, fettle, many with spectacular views; The Living Room Bar (above) and in-house Wave restaurant are quite a scene, the former with its own DJ; the rooftop Whiskey Sky bar is one of the city's indisputable hot spots, and there is an excellent, if busy, Bliss Spa for up-to-the-minute pampering. Plus it's near, if not exactly on, the beach.
644 N Lake Shore Drive, T 312 943 9200, www.whotels.com

The Peninsula

Since it opened in 2001, The Peninsula has out-luxed all of its peers. Holding a prime position on the Magnificent Mile, the opulence stretches over 20 floors. The top two are occupied by the city's most sophisticated spa and downtown's longest pool (see p092). The lofty-ceilinged lobby (left) exudes grandeur and, between 8.30pm and 11.30pm on Fridays and Saturdays, a resolve-melting aroma from a chocolate bar that offers 30 different cocoa-laced delights. Other treats include Shanghai Terrace, one of the best Asian restaurants in town. Some suites, such as The Peninsula (above), have studies and views over Lake Michigan; those on a lower budget might want to opt for a Junior Suite on the 18th floor.
108 E Superior Street, T 312 337 2888, chicago.peninsula.com

24 HOURS

SEE THE BEST OF THE CITY IN JUST ONE DAY

Few cities are as defined by their transport systems as Chicago is by the L, or elevated train. The first sections were built in 1892 and the system is now slow, overcrowded and in need of some serious investment. But it allows you to glide two storeys high – a rocking, rickety sort of glide – through the towers of The Loop and out into the various neighbourhoods, some hip and gentrified, others still tired and desperate places. A living city, spread out below you.

Our 24-hour schedule starts in the South Loop, an area definitely on the rise, and taking in Printers Row (see p026) – dangerous and desolate in the 1970s, now the focus of a loft-living revival. Check out the illustrated panels on the Franklin Building (720 S Dearborn Street). Next, it's south on the Green Line down to 35th-Bronzeville-IIT station, to see the stunning contributions Rem Koolhaas and Helmut Jahn have made – alongside or underneath the L – to Mies van der Rohe's Illinois Institute of Technology campus (see p027).

From there, it's back on the Green Line to head west. Stop for lunch at the excellent Italian restaurant Gioco (1312 S Wabash Avenue, T 312 939 3870) if you fancy, on your way to Oak Park (see p028), to see its amazing inventory of Frank Lloyd Wright houses. The day ends in River West, where the meatpacking warehouses are slowly being replaced by bars, restaurants and galleries. For better or worse, old Chicago is giving way to new Chicago.
For full addresses, see Resources.

08.30 Bongo Room

There's no shortage of good breakfast spots in Chicago, but the Bongo Room cafés take some beating. The S Wabash branch, with its brick and wood shell, cheerful nursery colour-scheme seating and super-fuelled menu is a fitting way to start a busy 24 hours. Pick up a *Tribune* and join South Loop residents for a laid-back morning feast – the most strenuous thing is making your choice. The pancakes are incredible and come with different offerings, such as banana and caramel or raspberry cream and lemon, according to the season. There's pear and cranberry French toast with caramel *gelato*, breakfast *burritos* or croissant sandwiches with herby sauté potatoes. The second hardest task is finishing the plate.

1152 S Wabash Avenue, T 312 291 0100, www.bongoroom.com

10.00 Printers Row

Work your way over to S Dearborn Street to enter a Chicago that feels strangely familiar, especially in the gloom of winter. So reminiscent of an early gangster movie are the streets, that on a quiet day you might feel like you are trespassing on set. Printers Row was once home to nearly 100 printing houses and many flophouses. After degeneration in the latter half of the 20th century, it picked up, and it is now the hub of the South Loop's loft-dwelling literati. Relics remain – of Chicago's six original stations, Dearborn is the last remaining terminal, while Kasey's Tavern (T 312 427 7992) has been pulling beers since 1889. Converted printhouses host newer bars and bookshops – unmissable is Sandmeyer's Bookstore (T 312 922 2104). *S Dearborn Street between W Congress Parkway and W Polk Street*

11.00 Tribune Campus, IIT

Mies van der Rohe put his money where his mouth was during his 20-year tenure as director of architecture at the Illinois Institute of Technology by designing its campus. But by the mid-1990s, even the IIT began to understand that man cannot live on (or in) Mies alone. Student numbers were down and the campus needed an architectural shot in the arm. Enter Rem Koolhaas, who won the prize to design the McCormick Tribune Student Center. He created a long, low building, seemingly squashed by the L train above, wrapped in a 160m corrugated steel and concrete tube. IIT also approached Helmut Jahn to design the State Street Village student dorms. Strung along the tracks of the L, the great stationary sleeper carriages punched with light-filled courtyards are a triumph.
3300 S Federal Street

16.00 Heurtley House, Oak Park

Ten miles west of The Loop, Oak Park is the Frank Lloyd Wright mother lode, with 25 Wright-designed residences built between 1889 and 1915. Wright built his own home and studio here (951 Chicago Avenue), which was restored in 1988, somewhat controversially, to the state he left it in 1909. Still, it makes for a fascinating tour. Not all of Wright's Oak Park houses merit too much attention – especially the early 'bootleg' buildings – but the 1902 Heurtley House stands out as one of his great works, the first Prairie Style house proper. Built for Chicago banker Arthur Heurtley, it has the same hunkered-down horizontalism as the later Robie House (see p060) and is perhaps even more beguiling. It's now a registered National Historic Landmark, but is not open to the public, sadly.
318 Forest Avenue

20.00 Timo

Timo's John Bubala is an owner-chef as you want an owner-chef to be: big, friendly and truly passionate about his food. Passionate and maybe a little promiscuous. After eight successful years at Thyme, serving French food, Bubala discovered a new culinary mistress. Tasting trips to Italy brought on a Pauline conversion and Bubala now serves up his own take on modern Italian, with an emphasis on wood-fired and rotisserie dishes. Try the wood-grilled romaine and pork shank served with butternut squash gnocchi with bacon and onions. To be sure, there are smarter interiors, but Timo has established itself as a favoured haunt of Chicago's media heavyweights, among others. It also has a fantastic patio.

464 N Halsted Street, T 312 226 4300, www.timochicago.com

23.00 Sonotheque

The best looking and best sounding club in town was designed by the in-demand Suhail, also responsible for the relaunched Lava Lounge (see p048) and the shortlived Del Toro in Wicker Park. The startling entrance is two storeys of large, powder-coated aluminium tiles, which reference the acoustic tiles dominating the interior; intact or sliced and artfully stacked, as they are in the entrance and behind the long quartz bar. The club itself is a long, half wood-lined, minimalist box. Corners are curved, to bounce the sound coming from the giant, backlit elevated speakers. The DJ booth is a sandblasted, glowing, glass sculpture but the overall effect is subdued and sophisticated. Try the sonic experience of Sunday's dub night.
1444 W Chicago Avenue, T 312 226 7600, www.sonotheque.net

URBAN LIFE

CAFÉS, RESTAURANTS, BARS AND NIGHTCLUBS

Foodies won't suffer in Chicago, but dieters might. The city has a generous quota of star chefs, the most celebrated being Charlie Trotter, and establishments that have won international acclaim, including Charlie Trotter's (816 W Armitage Avenue, T 773 248 6228) eponymous restaurant in Lincoln Park. A growing roster of Trotter's alumni is helping to buoy an ambitious scene, joining other local cooking heroes such as Ric Tramonto and Gale Gand of Tru (676 N Saint Clair Street, T 312 202 0001) and John Bubala of Timo (see p030). Molecular gastronomy has been embraced with gusto by many young chefs, notably Grant Achatz at Alinea (1723 N Halsted Street, T 312 867 0110) and Homaro Cantu of Moto (945 W Fulton Market, T 312 491 0058) – and here it's all about the theatre of the tasting menu. For our money, though, there's one foodie mogul who is ahead of the game. Donnie Madia's small empire, built with the help of chef Paul Kahan, includes the brilliant Blackbird (see p052), Avec (see p037) and Sonotheque (see p031).

Chicago does great neighbourhood eateries – Bourgeois Pig Café (738 W Fullerton Parkway, T 773 883 5282) is exemplary; old-school diners – try the Eleven City Diner (1112 S Wabash Avenue, T 312 212 1112); and steakhouses – Sullivan's (415 N Dearborn Street, T 312 527 3510) offers a traditional experience, while David Burke's Primehouse (see p018) serves up a more fashionably dressed slab. *For full addresses, see Resources.*

Marshall McGearty

If you miss the 'Smokers Allowed' sign in the window, this café-cum-bar is just a shabby-chic hangout offering fine pastries and coffee (and free wi-fi) by day and harder stuff in the evenings. But the frank encouragement to light up – there are vintage ashtrays everywhere, tobacco in jars, and odd-looking machines that staff use to make to-order cigarettes as quickly as a dry latte – makes it clear that this is designed as a smoker's shangri-la. The lounge is actually the first step of a slow-cooking plot by tobacco firm RJ Reynolds to build a premium cigarette business. Still, if you want to spark up (especially given the smoking ban in restaurants and bars, from which Marshall McGearty is exempt), this is the place to do it.
1553 N Milwaukee Avenue, T 773 772 8410, www.mmsmokes.com

Marshall McGearty

Green Zebra

It took three inspired food entrepreneurs in America's most carnivorous city to show that catering for vegetarians can be much more than a token gesture – it can be a supreme art. Since 2004, partners Peter Drohomyrecky and Sue Kim-Drohomyrecky and chef Shawn McClain have been offering a menu of small plates that will silence the most determined detractors of meatless cuisine.

The combinations are original but harmonious and the menu reads like poetry for the palate: creamy sunchoke ravioli, for example, with melted goat's cheese, hazelnuts and fresh dates. Situated in the partially regenerated Ukrainian Village district, it's doing plenty to draw the well-heeled into the neighbourhood. *1460 W Chicago Avenue, T 312 243 7100, www.greenzebrachicago.com*

Avec

All things considered – design, ambience, atmosphere, service and the sheer quality of the food – Avec is one of our favourite restaurants in the world. An almost severe cedarwood box with long bench and box seating, it's a no-reservation (and it does get mighty busy), squeeze-in-and-tuck-in sort of place, but the service, like the food, is designed to make you feel right at home. Try the chorizo-stuffed Medjool dates with smoked bacon and piquillo pepper-tomato sauce, followed by wood oven-roasted pork shoulder with knob onions, Cubanelle peppers and a chickpea *barigoule*. There's a great wine and cheese list, and the kitchen is open until midnight – turn up late and you'll find a huddle of the city's finest chefs and sommeliers eating here. *615 W Randolph Street, T 312 377 2002, www.avecrestaurant.com*

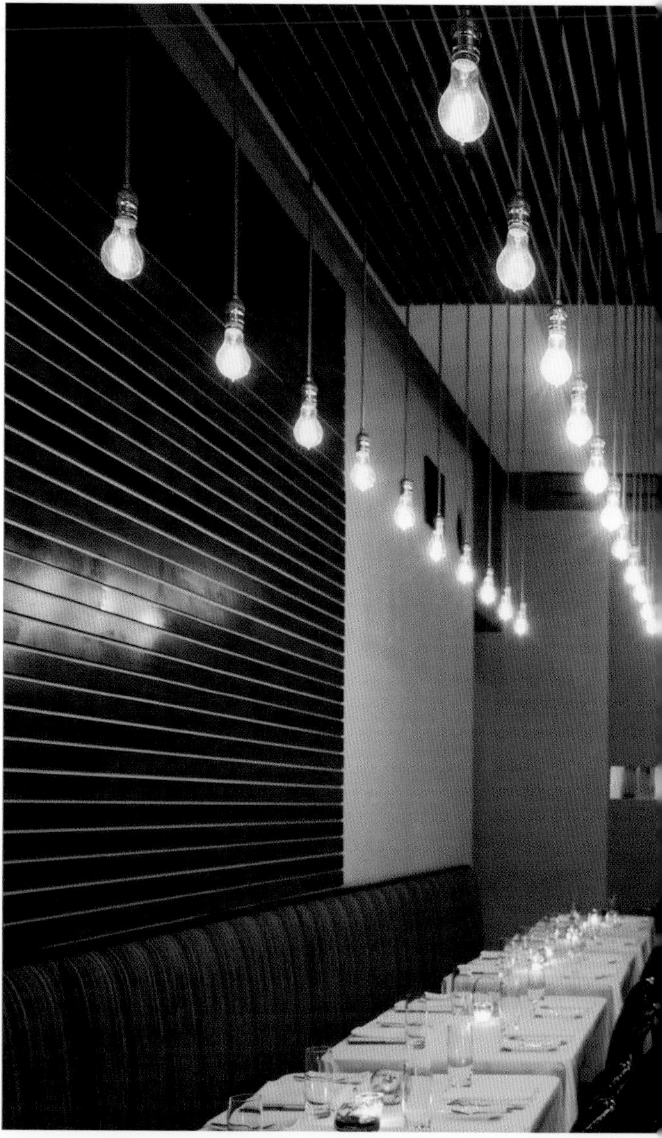

Aigre Doux

It's a brave restaurateur who takes on 230 W Kinzie Street. Many establishments have tried and failed to draw diners to this smudgy stretch overlooking the trade entrance of the Merchandise Mart. But Mohammed Islam and Malika Ameen, the owners of Aigre Doux, have an original story to tell and one that translates well into their food. Islam, a Bangladeshi who arrived in Chicago as an engineering student in 1986, has cooked at Chateau Marmont in LA and shows a commitment to perfection in his procedures that ensures his creations (say, pan-seared turbot with saffron sauce) are exceptional. His wife, Ameen, a pastry alumna of NYC's Balthazar, is responsible for mouthwatering desserts, such as sticky toffee pudding with Devonshire cream sorbet, and the bakery that greets you on arrival.
230 W Kinzie Street, T 312 329 9400, www.aigredouxchicago.com

Follia

There are pizzas aplenty in this town, but some of the best are served here. Follia exhibits all the typical touches of a contemporary Italian interior – glass mosaic tiles cover the central bar area, the walls are decorated with *stucco veneziano* and the furnishings are sleek and minimal. Delicious thin-crust pizzas emerge from a wood-burning oven at the back of the dining room,

while authentic Italian dishes – risottos, pastas, *scaloppine* and *caprese di bufala* are offered up as alternatives. And as though to authenticate further the Milanese provenance of its owners, Bruno and Melissa Abate, the work of young emerging fashion designers is exhibited in the window.

953 W Fulton Market, T 312 243 2888, www.folliachicago.com

Motel Bar

The design conceit at Hubie Greenwald's Near North hangout is, as the name suggests, mid-century motel – but it is delicately done. There is little in the way of kitsch or Rat Pack nonsense in this large industrial space, only smart, circular banquettes and comfortable sofas, a pool table and one of the best jukeboxes in town. Just as importantly, there is a great list of classic cocktails and an upmarket take on comfort food, such as hamburgers served with truffle aïoli, macaroni cheese and shepherd's pie. The kitchen is open until 1.30am (2.30am on Saturdays), so if you are hit with a late-night hankering for a Harvey Wallbanger and Buffalo wings while listening to The Clash or Thelonius Monk, this is the place.
600 W Chicago Avenue, T 312 822 2900,
www.themotelbar.com

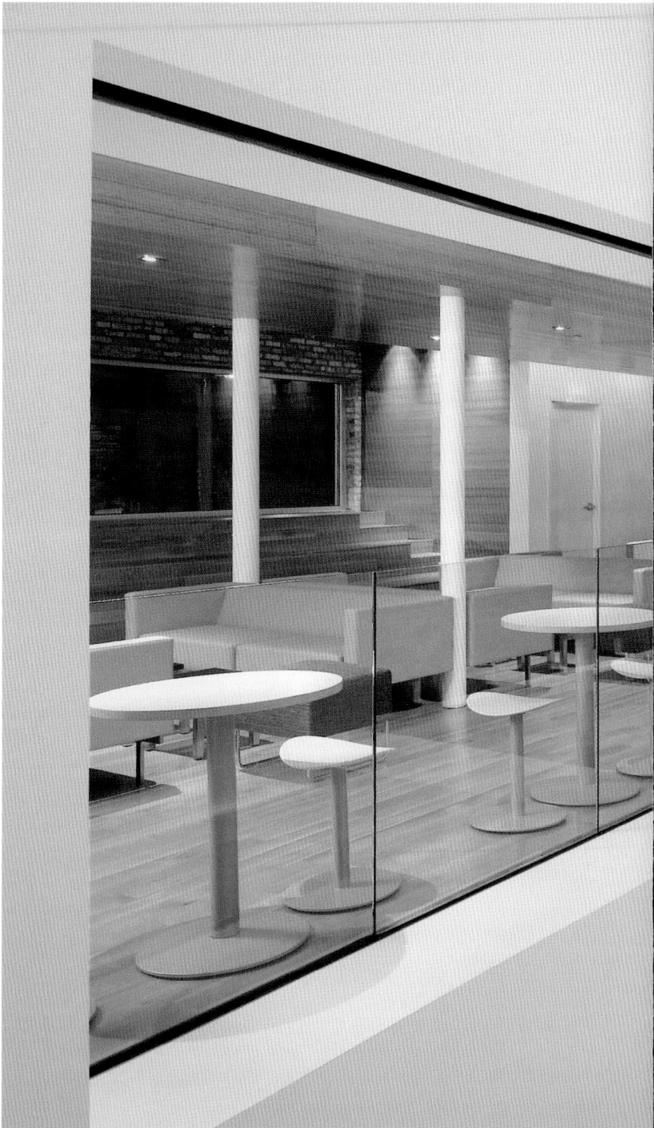

Saltaus

Nader Salti has stuck his neck out by converting this former corned-beef factory on the edges of the West Loop into an eating, drinking and dancing spot fit for smart, design-conscious urbanites. The bamboo-lined dining room offers a Mediterranean menu and the bar serves inventive cocktails.
1350 W Randolph Street, T 312 455 1919, www.saltaus.com

Sushi Wabi

The place that put industrial chic into Chicago's sushi scene, Sushi Wabi is not only the downtown design champ of the city's sushi houses – though Coast Sushi Bar (T 773 235 5775) comes close – it is also the best. The pristine bare-brick walls, exposed rafters, chunky wooden tabletops set on concrete and burnished-steel chairs make for an aggressively austere setting, but the food offers all the sensory stimulation you need. You know what you are going to get, though there are some off-piste elements to the menu. The *maki* is worth considering, and the crab-based 'spider' and 'tarantula' options tickled our fancy. Sushi Wabi also offers a good selection of sake, though they'll mix you a Martini if you want one. *842 W Randolph Street, T 312 563 1224, www.sushiwabi.com*

De Cero

Located in the city's most fashionable culinary corridor, De Cero shares the relaxed raw-urban aesthetic of its neighbours, with a hint of rustic in the scallop-edged benches and traditional wooden chairs. The dishes, too, display a similar medley, in this case of authentic Mexican and modern metropolitan. Chef Jill Barron describes the style as 'fresh coastal Mexican' – and the tacos and tamales certainly feature flavours that are faithful to a Pacific *taqueria*, but with small innovations and the freshest of local ingredients. There is an inventive cocktail menu full of fresh fruits and herbs, and a respectable tequila list too. *814 W Randolph Street, T 312 455 8114, www.decerotaqueria.com*

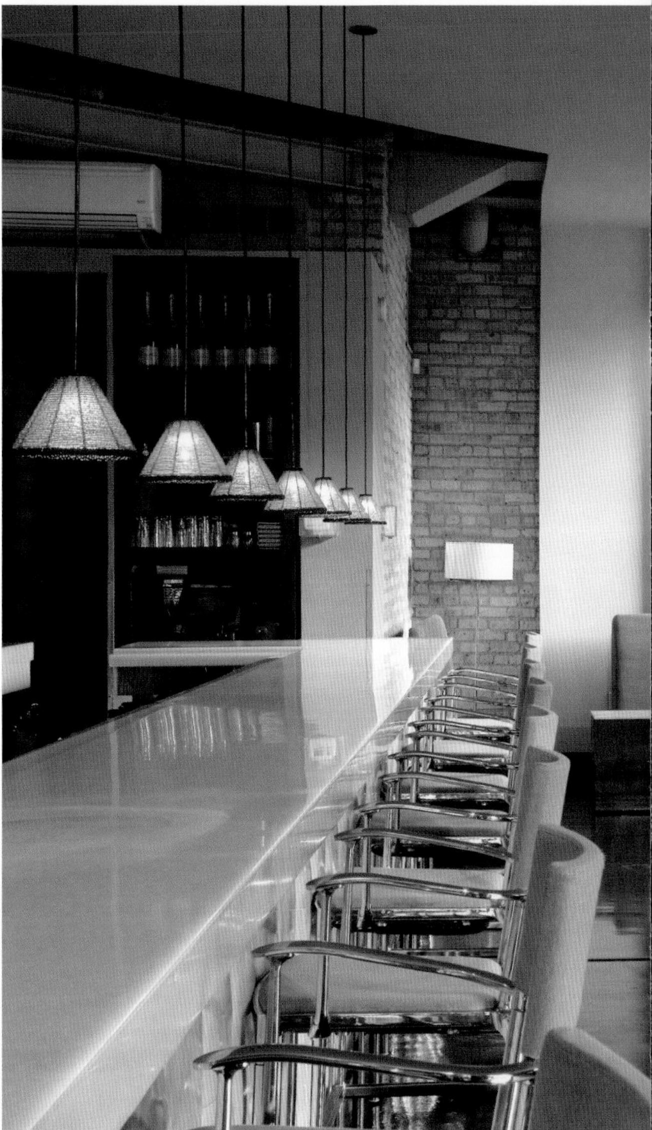

Fulton Lounge
Opened in 2002, the Fulton Lounge was
an early-comer to the regenerating Fulton
Market area. It sits among design galleries
and refrigeration plants, and feels very
much at home. Meatpackers may steer
clear, but nevertheless the atmosphere
is relaxed and lacking in pretension.
The former book-binding house features
vaulted ceilings, a black concrete floor,
brick walls, a long Avonite bar and vintage
tan punched-leather seating. It's a hub of
the neighbourhood and a good place to
get a sense of the new cultural community
that inhabits it – as well as a nightcap.
Drinks vary by season – in summer, when
the French windows are drawn back,
mojitos and sangria are on the menu; in
winter, caffeine-fuelled beverages by the
fireplace are more the scene.
955 W Fulton Market, T 312 942 9500,
www.fultonlounge.com

Lava Lounge

The original Lava Lounge was a well-loved agent of change in the Ukrainian Village, respected for its high-quality DJs and much lamented when it closed in 2006. Now the venue is back, in a new Wicker Park location and with a new look from local go-to designer Suhail. Owners Phil McFarland and Ty Fujimura run a relaxed, intimate ship, with a large and eclectic selection of beers to pickle yourself in, and have brought the original Lava's line-up of underground DJ talent with them. Like Sonotheque (see p031), also by Suhail, the all-new 170 sq m lounge makes use of acoustic tiles as design elements, but here the style is augmented by twisted red panels on the ceiling, honeycomb pendant lamps and smart leather banquettes.

1270 N Milwaukee Avenue, T 773 342 5282

One Sixty Blue

Michael Jordan's foray into fine dining is situated just a hop and a skip from Hoops The Gym (see p094), but the discreet nature of his involvement has meant that One Sixty Blue has stood on its own reputation since it opened in 1998, with chef Martial Noguier at the helm. Noguier came from apprenticeships with Alain Ducasse and Jacques Maximin in Monaco and his native France respectively, via stints working with esteemed chefs in Los Angeles and Washington DC. His style is traditional French cuisine modernised for an American audience. There are the odd extravagant flourishes, but his ingredients always favour local sources and seasonality, and the space keeps it elegantly understated.
1400 W Randolph Street, T 312 829 3046, www.onesixtyblue.com

Rodan

With a simple décor of blue banquettes, birchwood walls and a concrete floor, Rodan doesn't distinguish itself through its interior. But by juggling roles as a restaurant, music venue and gallery for video installations, it has found dedicated followers among the local music and art communities. A moderately priced menu of South American and Asian food is served thoughout the day, and a cocktail of drinks and DJs is served by night. Tuesday's jazz and improv night is highly recommended. This is where you'll catch local musicians such as John Herndon (of Tortoise), Josh Abrams and Nori Tanaka hashing it out for a few sets.
1530 N Milwaukee Avenue, T 773 276 7036, www.rodan.ws

Hot Chocolate

Whereas Marshall McGearty (see p033) is dedicated to the joys of smoking, Hot Chocolate is committed to a sweeter vice. The particular Wonka behind this Bucktown confectioner's is Mindy Segal, former pastry chef at the highly respected MK The Restaurant (T 312 482 9179). Of course it delivers on the promise of its name, offering almost certainly the best hot chocolate you have ever tasted, and its desserts are legendary. But Hot Chocolate's mains are good enough to turn this into a well-rounded restaurant experience. The interior doesn't lay on the sweet stuff too thickly, either, but is nicely done out in various chocolatey tones.
1747 N Damen Avenue, T 773 489 1747, www.hotchocolatechicago.com

Blackbird

In design terms, Blackbird is a kind of deluxe version of Avec (see p037) – it's a similarly chic and minimal long box, but here you get mohair banquettes, a cinematic open kitchen and a very elegant private dining room. The food is highest-quality modern American with light dollops of Frenchness.
619 W Randolph Street, T 312 715 0708, www.blackbirdrestaurant.com

INSIDER'S GUIDE

JIHA LEE, FASHION STORE MANAGER

Lee has worked as the store manager at Hejfina (see p083) for three years, and undertakes music and art projects in her spare time. Her favourite galleries include Shane Campbell (1431 W Chicago Avenue, T 312 226 2223) and The Suburban out in Oak Park (244 W Lake Street, T 708 763 8554), which puts on 'some of the most interesting exhibitions in Chicago'.

For food shopping and delicious soups at lunchtime, Lee drops in to Olivia's Market (see p072). 'It always has what I need, from Vosges chocolate and squid-ink pasta to good wines and cheese.' For fresh produce, she heads to Stanley's Fruit & Vegetables (1558 N Elston Avenue, T 773 276 8050). In the evenings, Lee mostly hangs out at Rodan (see p050), where she has also moonlighted as a host, for its laid-back vibe, nightly DJs and moderately priced menu and drinks list. She also likes the teeny-tiny bar Matchbox (770 N Milwaukee Avenue, T 312 666 9292), where she orders Martinis, and Skylark (2149 S Halsted Street, T 312 948 5275), which serves great hamburgers and Tater Tots (hash browns) with three dipping sauces: 'Excess at its best/worst.'

A live music fan, her favourite local bands are The Ponys, Pit Er Pat and Andrew Bird – catch them at venues like The Empty Bottle (1035 N Western Avenue, T 773 276 3600) or The Hideout (1354 W Wabansia Avenue, T 773 227 4433).

For full addresses, see Resources.

ARCHITOUR

A GUIDE TO CHICAGO'S ICONIC BUILDINGS

In 1871, much of Chicago was destroyed by fire. For a city already committed to challenging New York as the commercial (if not cultural) epicentre of the nation, this provided Chicago with the opportunity to rebuild itself as a thrusting metropolis, and architects poured in from all over the country to be part of the grand project. Among them were Louis Sullivan – who gave the world the maxim 'form follows function' – William Le Baron Jenney, Daniel Burnham and his partner John Root. They developed what became known as the Chicago School and built the first skyscrapers here. Though they barely scraped into double digits, storey-wise, these buildings were, in their steel-frame construction and emphasis on functional styling, the technical parents of the giants to come.

Chicago seems to provide textbook illustrations of successive architectural styles – the city gave the world the vertical thrust of the skyscraper and the horizontal planes of Frank Lloyd Wright's Prairie School; it was the mother lode of modernism and became a PoMo playground – and these shifts from style to style can appear seamless. Of course, the development of Chicago's architecture has always been the result of a fierce and chaotic contest of different approaches and interests – sometimes in the same building. It is the quality of the contest that makes Chicago the city where 20th-century architecture finds its most perfect form.

For full addresses, see Resources.

John Hancock Center

One firm, Skidmore, Owings & Merrill, has dominated corporate architecture in postwar America. Nowhere is that dominance more evident than in Chicago. And no building better exemplifies SOM's power slabs than the John Hancock Center, completed in 1970. Largely the work of Myron Goldsmith, the uncompromising criss-cross trusses and black aluminium skin of the tapered 400m-high, 100-storey tower give it a brooding, iconic force and make it the definitive Chicago building. The John Hancock Center marks one end of the Magnificent Mile and the open-air viewing deck on the 94th floor is the best place to take in views of not just Chicago but an impressive portion of the Midwest.
875 N Michigan Avenue

Millennium Park

The city's latest landmark, Millennium Park, is set over 10ha and is dominated by massive sculptural statements, not least of which is Frank Gehry's Jay Pritzker Pavilion (pictured). It looks exactly as you would expect a Gehry open-air auditorium to look: giant steel petals and an intricate piping canopy. It plays perfectly to the architect's strengths and is a stunner.
www.millenniumpark.org

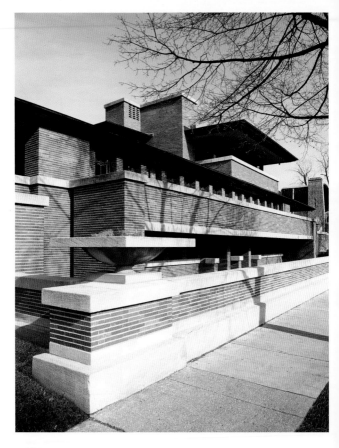

Robie House

Built in 1910, the Robie House is the most famous and fully realised of Frank Lloyd Wright's Prairie houses. Frederick Robie was a bicycle-factory owner – a forward-thinking entrepreneur who wanted the most futuristic house possible. And the one Wright designed and built for him was revolutionary, not least in having a garage connected to the house, burglar alarms and a built-in vacuum cleaner. The Robie House still looks like an angular, futuristic ship dry-docked in one of the swankiest parts of south Chicago. Everything, even down to the choice of brick, is designed to emphasise horizontal planes. The building, which is open to the public, is in the midst of a £4.5m restoration and the exterior now glows clean and red.

5757 S Woodlawn Avenue, T 708 848 1976, www.wrightplus.org

Xerox Center

Completed in 1980, the Xerox Center was Helmut Jahn's first major development in Chicago, and the building where the German-born architect made his first tentative – and very successful – steps away from the modernist box. Jahn's simple trick was to round off one of the corners of the building and set it back from the pavement, giving real drama to the 41-storey glass tower – it has to compete with the immense Chase Tower (see p066), which stands across the road. The windows on the north façade are much larger than those facing east, adding to a sense of elegant rupture with the straight-up slabs of the past.
55 W Monroe Street

The Rookery

At the end of the 19th century, Chicago was a Beijing or Shanghai; architects moved there to build a new metropolis. Among them were Daniel Burnham and John Root. The Rookery, completed in 1888, is their finest and most influential work. The tallest building in the world when it was finished, the Rookery's exterior is an extraordinary mix of Venetian, Moorish and Byzantine influences. But it is Root's interior that was truly radical. An atrium and large lightwell allowed for an indoor shopping arcade – the first in the world. The lobby boasts elaborate staircases, ornamental rails and intricately carved marble panels. Frank Lloyd Wright renovated the central courtyard in 1905, and the building has been beautifully restored after falling into disrepair.
209 S LaSalle Street

CNA Plaza

Even if no one actually knows what it is called, CNA Plaza is one of the best known and best loved of all Chicago's corporate towers. Completed in 1972, the building is a 44-storey slab, a very confident take on the stark International Style. Had architects Graham, Anderson, Probst & White or their clients gone for the style's trademark Miesian black, the Plaza would have been just as fine but largely ignored. But it's not black – it's a bright (if rusty) red, and as such seems a gift to the skyline, a building of quiet elegance that refuses to fade into the background. Its windows are often lit up to signal messages of holiday cheer and suchlike.
325 S Wabash Avenue

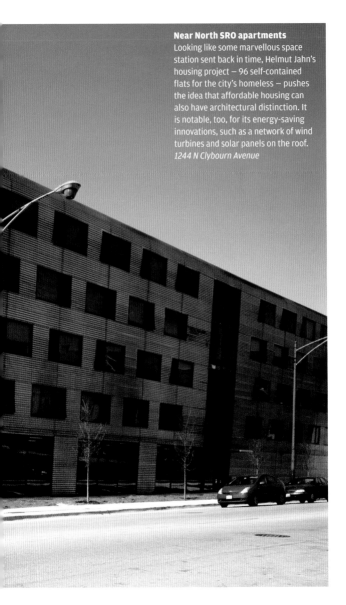

Near North SRO apartments
Looking like some marvellous space station sent back in time, Helmut Jahn's housing project – 96 self-contained flats for the city's homeless – pushes the idea that affordable housing can also have architectural distinction. It is notable, too, for its energy-saving innovations, such as a network of wind turbines and solar panels on the roof.
1244 N Clybourn Avenue

Chase Tower

As many great buildings as there are in Chicago, there are also a good many clunkers. Luckily, the central block of The Loop, a symbolic focal point, is occupied by one of the city's most graceful and dramatic constructions. Chase Tower (originally the First National Bank Building and pretty soon after, Bank One Plaza) was designed by CF Murphy Associates and Perkins + Will and completed in 1969.

Essentially a 60-storey modernist slab, its intense visual drama comes from an elegant sweep from the base, which starts at 60m wide, to the top, where the building ends up only half that. The tower is also known for the two-storey sunken plaza to its south – it includes Marc Chagall's *Four Seasons*, a mosaic rendered in 370 sq m of ceramic tiles.

10 S Dearborn Street

Lake Point Tower

Completed in 1968, Lake Point Tower is still one of Chicago's most chic addresses, and its design is as compelling as it was then. Essentially the 70-storey tower has a triangular plan with bowed sides. All supports and services are at the core, meaning that each of the promontories needs no interior load-bearing walls, allowing for complete freedom of design. All of the apartments manage to get a view of Lake Michigan but, thanks to the curvature of the windows, not of other residents' apartments. The building also boasts a 10,000 sq m private park on the third floor. Designed by the landscape architect Alfred Caldwell, it includes an outdoor swimming pool, a waterfall and lagoon, manicured gardens and 80 trees. *505 N Lake Shore Drive, www.lakepointtower.org*

Metropolitan Correctional Center

Possibly the single most startling structure in all of Chicago, which is saying something, the Metropolitan Correctional Center is a slit-windowed fortress of the future, the prison from a grim science-fiction movie landed at the southern edge of The Loop. Designed by Harry Weese, who is also responsible for the metro system in Washington DC, and completed in 1975, it is an innovative 27-storey triangular concrete wedge (although the prison only occupies 16 floors; the rest of the building is office space). At the time, it represented the latest in correctional best practice and compassionate incarceration – the design meant that all cells had windows but could also be near the facility's well-appointed communal areas – but it still comes off as thoroughly dystopian. In a cool way.

71 W Van Buren Street

Fisher Studio Houses

Still a startlingly successful splice of deco design and modernist mechanics, the Fisher Studio Houses were constructed in 1938 by Andrew Rebori, a noted *bon vivant* who had useful relations with the Chicago social élite. The building was commissioned by Frank Fisher, an executive at Marshall Fields, who showed Rebori a very narrow plot and told him to get the most upscale apartments he could out of it. He came up with 12 four-storey duplexes built around a courtyard. They were fronted by an elegant painted brick and rounded glass-brick façade – typical of the 'Depression modern' school, with sculptural flourishes by the artist Edgar Miller. Indeed, there is some suspicion that Miller had a larger hand in the building's design and it remains a thrilling composition face-on.
1209 N State Parkway

Gary Comer Youth Center
Situated in the tough Grand Crossing
neighbourhood, the Gary Comer Youth
Center was designed as an inspirational
symbol and resource for a community
still struggling with big problems. Most
of the building is made up of long blue
or red panelled bricks – one of the
instructions architect John Ronan was
given was not to use too much glass.
7200 S Ingleside Avenue

SHOPPING

THE BEST RETAIL THERAPY AND WHAT TO BUY

Strangers to Chicago might anticipate a paucity of unique retail opportunities. It does, after all, sit atop the country's conservative heartland. But much of what gives the city its identity, including its position as command centre of the Midwest, also makes it a robust shopping destination. A playground for the world's architects throughout the 20th century and beyond, Chicago has become a mecca for enthusiasts of mid-century design, while its thriving restaurant culture has put gastro-gadgetry firmly on the shopping agenda. We recommend a trip to Bloomingdale's Home Store (600 N Wabash Avenue, T 312 324 7500), an ornate temple that was once home to the local Shriners movement, while curious cooks should look to neighbourhood grocers such as Olivia's Market (2014 W Wabansia Avenue, T 773 227 4220); coffee (see p077) and chocolate (see p082) are bona fide souvenirs. As you'd expect, Chicago has a rich seam of music stores and excellent bookshops (see p078).

Shopping in the city can be largely separated into areas. For independent fashion and delis, Wicker Town, Bucktown and Lake View are best. For design, head to the West Loop. For art of the established variety, River North is the place, while Peoria Street offers a more contemporary scene. The south end of The Loop has independent bookstores, and for upscale fashion, stroll along the Magnificent Mile and wallet-weakening area around Oak Street. *For full addresses, see Resources.*

Pavilion

Deborah Colman and Neil Kraus made this 120 sq m showroom home to their design gallery business in 1996. Graduates of the Art Institute of Chicago, they discovered a mutual passion for mid-century French furnishings, lighting and ceramics, which they collect on frequent trips to Europe. Although rarities by the likes of Perriand, Prouvé and Paulin may be their holy grail, their inventory also includes interesting Italian and Scandinavian pieces, and even sympathetic designs from earlier centuries. It's worth checking the owners' slightly itinerant schedule online before making a special trip here, as opening times and stock are often in a state of flux.
2055 N Damen Avenue, T 773 645 0924, www.pavilionantiques.com

Wright Gallery
Some of the rarest pieces of modernist
design go under the hammer in this airy
one-time printing house on the outer
reaches of the West Loop. Here you can
bid on an original Paul Kjaerholm coffee
table, a Robert Mallet-Stevens armchair,
a 356 Speedster Porsche or even a Pierre
Koenig Case Study house.
1440 W Hubbard Street, T 312 563 0020,
www.wright20.com

Modern Times

Occupying a vast brick-walled warehouse space, Modern Times is at the western frontier of the design district. Tom Clark and Martha Torno opened their gallery of 20th-century design back in 1991, and their hoard remains as strong as ever. Heavy on American mid-century modern lighting, ceramics and furnishings by the likes of Norman Bel Geddes, this impressive collection is low on design clichés, and high on brilliant finds, and everything on sale is in tip-top condition. A personal passion for vintage accessories is reflected in the couple's sideline: bags and jewels (www.modbag.com) picked up on foraging missions around the world. It's certainly worth trekking out here, even though it does feel a little out on a limb. *2100 W Grand Avenue, T 312 243 5706, www.moderntimeschicago.com*

Metropolis Coffee

There's a rich coffee culture in Chicago. The brand Intelligentsia rules the roasts, and rounds off meals in the city's most prestigious eating establishments. It thoroughly deserves its reputation, but we have also discovered the delicious and pleasingly packaged Metropolis line, which consists of organic blends named Ottoman Adventure (above), £13.25 per kg, Redline Espresso and Samba, along with seasonal specials, all of which are hand-roasted and packed in the heart of the city. Both brands can be picked up in the delightfully named deli, The Goddess and Grocer (T 773 342 3200).
www.metropoliscoffee.com

Prairie Avenue Bookshop
This isn't a city short on voracious readers or bookstores, nor are its streets lacking in monumental architecture. It comes as little surprise, then, that it is home to one of our favourite architectural bookshops. Located below a clunking L-train viaduct, the Prairie Avenue Bookshop was opened in 1961 by Marilyn and Wilbert Hasbrouck, who also published *The Prairie School Review*, dedicated to Frank Lloyd Wright and his disciples (back issues can be bought here). An air of academia hangs over this comprehensive library of design literature – some 22,000 titles, both in and out of print – though it's not above the retail of cards, maps, games and related tchotchkes. Dominating the second level is a large reading table circled by high-backed chairs (right), where you can test out the wares before you invest.
418 S Wabash Avenue, T 312 922 8311, www.pabook.com

Koros

Tucked away on one of the less trampled streets of the West Loop's meatpacking district, Koros is a destination, word-of-mouth fashion store. It has an airy, warehouse feel, and is furnished with vintage wardrobes and chairs, ambient lighting and glass bricks (a design detail that pervades the city). Opening times are odd, but a glass of champagne – offered even to mere browsers – makes up for it.

Owner Kristen Skordilis travels the world in search of rare, unusual and just brilliant fashion finds each season – some names are more familiar than others. Currently there is clothing from Clu, Hoss, Tori Nichel and J Lindeberg, jeans from Edun, BYA and Earnest Sewn and beauty products from Anthousa and Sundari.
1019 W Lake Street, T 312 738 0155, www.korosartandstyle.com

Casati

Open since 2003, the Casati gallery is the kingpin of the ever-evolving design district centred around the West Loop. Focusing on sculpture and art as well as lighting and furniture by mid-century Italian masters, it is a fitting complement to stores such as Pavilion (see p073), Modern Times (see p076) and the Wright Gallery (see p074). Owner Ugo Alfano Casati secures a steady flow of items by 20th-century Italian design luminaries, including Gio Ponti, Carlo Molino, Joe Colombo and Gaetano Pesce, and has earned an international following due to the quality and focus of his collection. *949 W Fulton Street, T 312 421 9905, www.casatigallery.com*

Coco Rouge

Chocolate suppliers are not wanting in the Windy City – the now internationally renowned Vosges chocolates originated here, The Peninsula's lobby (see p022) has a spectacular Chocolate Bar, and cocoa chains such as Ethel's Chocolate Lounge warm Chicagoan cockles through those challenging winters. Coco Rouge, one of the most recent to appear, sweetens up the south edge of Wicker Park, offering a menu of hot chocolate beverages to be consumed at the low tables to the front of the store. Cocoa-based confectionery is conjured up by the resident chocolatier, who can be seen at work in the industrial kitchen behind the counter. Boxed in beautifully styled wooden cases, sealed with wax, they make a great souvenir. *1940 W Division Street, T 773 772 2626, www.cocorouge.com*

Hejfina

The perfect 21st-century store, Hejfina fills an airy, well-placed space with menswear and womenswear, furniture, books on art and architecture, tabletop pieces and accessories. The furniture collection comes courtesy of local designers Carson Maddox and Koehler Design Build, whose designs are perfect examples of minimalist functionality (both offer a custom design service through Hejfina); glassware is by Chicagoan studio F2. Hejfina's fashion stable runs the gamut from Comme des Garçons to niche lines such as Tsumori Chisato and Alice Ritter, and there is an interesting mix of local and international jewellery. The space serves as an artistic hub too, hosting installations and talks on art and architecture.
1529 N Milwaukee Avenue, T 773 772 0002, www.hejfina.com

Apartment No 9

The cherry-wood and concrete interior of Apartment No 9, by Koehler Design Build, sets the tone – the décor combines antique *objets*, such as an old post-office cabinet, with smart modern trimmings made of leather. It's a boutique for an emerging breed of Chicagoan man who sees beyond the baseball cap and chinos; he has an appreciation of quality and heritage, but a modern sensibility when it comes to materials and silhouette. Brands stocked include Coast, Martin Margiela, Dries Van Noten, Paul Smith and Etro. The near-inevitable library of grooming products includes stock by John Allan's and The Art of Shaving.
1804 N Damen Avenue, T 773 395 2999

Morlen Sinoway

On the north side of W Fulton Market is a small strip of contemporary design stores worth close inspection. Function and Art (www.functionart.com) has an unusual mix of pieces by featured artists and designers scouted internationally. Morlen Sinoway offers a more accessible collection of furniture and tabletop pieces from a fold of internationally important design houses. This is where to pick up a Wendell Castle 'Snap' table (above), £1,860, Hans Wegner chair, Vincent Van Duysen pottery, Carlo Moretti glassware or a Kasthall rug. But those with a spirit of adventure will check out the distinctive work of Sinoway himself, an artist and designer who custom-makes furniture and consults on interiors around the city. *1052 W Fulton Market, T 312 432 0100, www.morlensinoway.com*

Salvage One
Combine the cool of a design gallery
with the exciting unpredictability of
a junk store, and you get Salvage One.
It's an architectural-reclaim business
founded by a Sotheby's veteran, which
offers up everything from church pews
to an old dentist's chair and furnishings
that span the 20th century – at a price.
*1840 W Hubbard Street, T 312 733 0098,
www.salvageone.com*

SPORTS AND SPAS
WORK OUT, CHILL OUT OR JUST WATCH

To the uninitiated, the sporting landscape of Chicago may appear to be populated by a lot of animals you wouldn't want to encounter on a dark night: cubs, bears, wolves and bulls. But these are the stars of the city's stadia. The Cubs (homeground: Wrigley Field, opposite) and White Sox (Comiskey Park) are the leading baseball teams; the Bears are blue-collar Chicago's representatives on the gridiron; the Wolves play ice hockey; and the Bulls are the basketball team that won six consecutive NBA titles in the 1990s. The stadia themselves hold their own too, arguably featuring the best of the old in Wrigley Field and the best of the new in the 2003 renovation of Soldier Field (1410 S Museum Campus Drive, T 312 235 7000).

When it comes to everyday corporal honing, the city offers parks and lakeshore trails to runners, cyclers and skaters. Gyms and spas are plentiful, if undistinguished in design. The pool at the Four Seasons (see p020) does a great line in throwaway swimming costumes and has an enviable ceiling view, but The Peninsula Spa pool (see p092) is better for racking up lengths. As for spas, Ruby Room (1743-45 W Division Street, T 773 235 2323) is deservedly popular, while Bliss (644 N Lake Shore Drive, T 312 201 9545) is a polished pampering retreat. Trim (see p090) and the West Loop Gym (see p093) are less predictable and satisfy our desire to feel a sense of place even when being waxed or working out.
For full addresses, see Resources.

Wrigley Field

One of the country's oldest and best loved ballparks, Wrigley Field was built in 1914 for a now defunct Federal League team, the Whales. The architect, Zachary Taylor Davis, was a contemporary of Frank Lloyd Wright, with whom he worked as a draughtsman for Louis Sullivan. This commission and a previous one (the original Comiskey Park for the White Sox) earned him the moniker 'the Frank Lloyd Wright of baseball'. Previously, ballparks had been more temporary wooden structures; Davis introduced steel beams and concrete. Renovated and expanded by chewing-gum magnate William Wrigley Jr in the 1920s, the ivy-covered, asymmetric, advertisement-free stadium has changed little since the 1940s and is still the envy of other clubs.
1060 W Addison Street, T 773 404 2827

Trim

We love the fact that even a waxing
service can absorb local colour and
character. The mid-century mood here
includes vintage cabinets and David
Hicks wallpaper, while the pampering
treatments for men and women include
eyebrow-threading and brightening up
parts that never usually see the light.
*2503 N Lincoln Avenue, T 773 525 8746,
www.trimwax.com*

The Peninsula Spa

The esteemed Peninsula hotel (see p022) can't rest on its laurels without risking a tumble. Which explains why, within five years of the hotel's launch in 2001, the in-house spa underwent an extensive rejig to transform it into one of the city's most impressive and enticing urban retreats. The serene space occupies the top two floors of the building. The reception and treatment areas are wrapped in wood, a high-tech gym surveys Lake Michigan, from a distance of 19 floors, and the Olympic-length pool (above) is downtown's longest and sunniest. There is a terrace for summer idling, a yoga studio and treatment rooms offering therapies and massage using Espa products. The spa is open to non-guests Monday to Thursday. *108 E Superior Street, T 312 573 6860, chicago.peninsula.com*

West Loop Gym

This is the gym that you've modelled in your dreams when overstyled temples to fitness have sent you running to the hills (or to the local park, at least). West Loop is a neighbourhood gym with an atmosphere that is about as relaxed as you can get in a place where people spin, kick, tread and tone. The converted warehouse has a lofty feel with exposed beams, bricks and wooden floors. There's a range of fitness facilities and classes, including FreeMotion circuit training, cardiovascular equipment, spinning, yoga, Pilates and kickboxing. It puts an emphasis on 'functional fitness': a holistic, needs-based sort of regime. So sensible. Staff are friendly and helpful, and on hand if a personal session is required. Day passes are available to non-members. *1024 W Kinzie Street, T 312 421 8573, www.westloopgym.net*

Hoops The Gym
This private basketball gymnasium
is another legendary sporting venue,
even though it has existed only since
1992. Then again, the basketball player
who gave the gym its mythical status
was only just getting going in 1992.
Also known as 'the house that Michael
Jordan built', Hoops was founded by
Gary Cowen, who was soon partnered
by Tim Grover, Jordan's personal trainer,
and it immediately became the training
ground for scores of world-famous NBA
stars, including 'Magic' Johnson, Larry
Bird and, of course, local basketball
deity Jordan himself. It can be hired by
amateur mortals for personal training,
group sessions and social events for £55
an hour when the pros are out of town.
1001 W Washington Boulevard,
T 312 850 9496

ESCAPES

WHERE TO GO IF YOU WANT TO LEAVE TOWN

Despite Chicago's status as one of the world's busiest aviation hubs, few think of it as a base for shorter jaunts. This is despite the fact that much of the surrounding country is not the flat, grassy prairie of legend, but rather hills and beaches and sand dunes and great pine forests. It is no accident that immigrant Scandinavians have found such comfort in the local landscape. Visitors also have four states to investigate: Illinois, Michigan, Wisconsin and Indiana, each with its own particular and peculiar history. Berrien County, 150km to the north-east, has become a focal point for Michigan's surprisingly vibrant viticulture. Nearby Harbor County boasts the upscale New Buffalo lakeside resort. Madison, Wisconsin's capital, is famous for its 200 parks, five lakes, 13 beaches, fine food, vigorous cultural life and all-round liveability. And all just 230km away.

The Midwest also does a nice line in built environment. It's as if all the architectural energy expended on Chicago spread, from Mies van der Rohe's pristine Farnsworth House (see p102) in Plano, Illinois, and Frank Lloyd Wright's monumental efforts in Racine, Wisconsin (see p100), to the unique result of corporate benevolence in Columbus, Indiana (opposite and overleaf). If that isn't enough, there's Santiago Calatrava's Milwaukee Art Museum (700 N Art Museum Drive, Milwaukee, T 414 224 3200). And you thought all the city had to offer was beer and *Laverne & Shirley*.

For full addresses, see Resources.

Columbus, Indiana

Despite having a population of just 39,000, Columbus, 360km south-east of Chicago, was recently anointed as the sixth most architecturally significant city in the US. In 1957, the town's major employer, the Cummins Engine Co (run by J Irwin Miller, the 'Medici of the Midwest'), decided it would cover the design fees for a series of public buildings, as long as architects of international standing and modernist intent were recruited. There had been a precursor in the town: Eero Saarinen's 1954 Irwin Union Bank (above; 500 Washington Street), which broke the mould for finance buildings in the US. To date, Columbus has more than 60 buildings of architectural interest, including work by Robert Venturi, Richard Meier, Robert Stern and IM Pei.

Irwin Union Bank, Columbus
Columbus (see p097) is no museum, and
the quality just keeps coming. In 2006,
architect Deborah Berke's sublime Irwin
Union Bank was opened, breathing new
life into a commercial strip dominated
by empty parking lots. This is not your
average American town – Columbus
boasts two universities, two symphony
orchestras and 15 public parks.
707 Creekview Drive

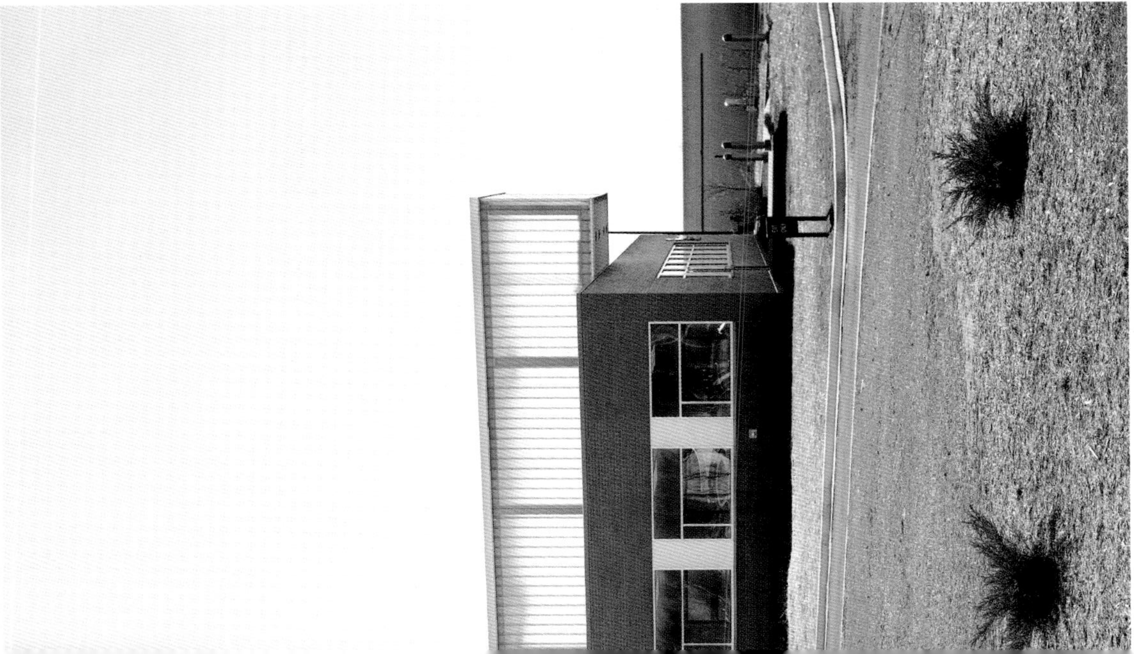

Johnson Wax Building, Racine

Despite a reputation as a huge, if irascible, architectural talent, by the mid-1930s work had become thin on the ground for Frank Lloyd Wright. He was rescued by Herbert Johnson of SC Johnson & Son, the wax people, who commissioned him to build new offices, and a mansion, in the pleasant lakeside town of Racine, Wisconsin. Completed in 1939, the office building is a squat, corporate-sized take on the Prairie Style, and became known for its mushrooming, 9.5m internal columns (left). Despite the famous Wright temper, Johnson returned to him in order to design a research facility. Wright came up with a 15-storey tower (above), opened in 1950, which is still a wonder to behold, but proved largely useless for its purpose, and was closed after three decades.

1525 Howe Street, T 262 260 2154

Farnsworth House, Plano

Mies van der Rohe never got more Miesian (or more grief) than he did for Farnsworth House, completed in 1951. The client was Dr Edith Farnsworth, a Chicago kidney specialist who asked Mies to design and build her a country house on a 25ha plot of bucolic loveliness on the Fox River in Plano, Illinois. He came up with a sublime floating glazed box, just 22.5 by 8.5m, held aloft by white steel I-beams. Not that Dr Farnsworth was pleased. She kicked Mies off the job before he had completed the interiors and then sued for incompetence. There is, however, some suspicion that the relationship between Mies and the good doctor went beyond the professional, and that she was far from pleased when the master architect's ardour cooled. *14520 River Road, T 630 552 0052, www.farnsworthhouse.org*

Dear Reader, books by Phaidon are recognized worldwide for their beauty, scholarship and elegance. We invite you to return this card with your name and e-mail address so that we can keep you informed of our new publications, special offers and events. Alternatively, visit us at **www.phaidon.com** to see our entire list of books, videos and stationery. Register on-line to be included on our regular e-newsletters.

Subjects in which I have a special interest

☐ General Non-Fiction ☐ Art ☐ Photography ☐ Architecture ☐ Design

☐ Fashion ☐ Music ☐ Children's ☐ Food ☐ Travel

| Mr/Miss/Ms | Initial | Surname |

Name

No./Street

City — Country

Postcode/Zip code

E-mail

This is not an order form. To order please contact Customer Services at the appropriate address overleaf.

Please delete address not required before mailing

PHAIDON PRESS INC.
180 Varick Street
New York
NY 10014
USA

PHAIDON PRESS LIMITED
Regent's Wharf
All Saints Street
London N1 9PA
UK

Return address for USA and Canada only

*Return address for UK and countries
outside the USA and Canada only*

*Affix
stamp
here*

NOTES

SKETCHES AND MEMOS

RESOURCES

CITY GUIDE DIRECTORY

HOTELS

ADDRESSES AND ROOM RATES

Hotel Burnham 016
Room rates:
double, from $300
1 W Washington Street
T 312 782 1111
www.burnhamhotel.com

Four Seasons 020
Room rates:
double, from $600;
Deluxe Executive Suite, $900;
Author Suite, $1,700
120 E Delaware Place
T 312 280 8800
www.fourseasons.com

InterContinental 016
Room rates:
double, from $150
505 N Michigan Avenue
T 312 944 4100
www.icchicagohotel.com

The James 018
Room rates:
double, from $300;
Loft Suite, from $400
55 E Ontario Street
T 312 337 1000
www.jameshotels.com

Park Hyatt 016
Room rates:
double, from $460
800 N Michigan Avenue
T 312 335 1234
www.parkchicago.hyatt.com

The Peninsula 022
Room rates:
double, from $525;
Junior Suite, from $925;
The Peninsula Suite, $7,500
108 E Superior Street
T 312 337 2888
chicago.peninsula.com

The Ritz-Carlton 016
Room rates:
double, from $480
160 E Pearson Street
T 312 266 1000
www.fourseasons.com/chicagorc

Sofitel 016
Room rates:
double, from $175
20 E Chestnut Street
T 312 324 4000
www.sofitel.com

W Chicago City Center 017
Room rates:
double, from $200
172 W Adams Street
T 312 332 1200
www.whotels.com

W Chicago Lakeshore 021
Room rates:
double, from $200
644 N Lake Shore Drive
T 312 943 9200
www.whotels.com

WALLPAPER* CITY GUIDES

Editorial Director
Richard Cook

Art Director
Loran Stosskopf

City Editors
Nick Compton
Emma Moore

Editor
Rachael Moloney

Executive Managing Editor
Jessica Firmin

Travel Bookings Editor
Sara Henrichs

Chief Designer
Benjamin Blossom

Designer
Daniel Shrimpton

Map Illustrator
Russell Bell

Photography Editor
Christopher Lands

Photography Assistant
Robin Key

Chief Sub-Editor
Jeremy Case

Sub-Editors
Catriona Luke
Stephen Patience

Assistant Sub-Editor
Milly Nolan

Interns
Clare Roberts
Lizzy Tinley

Wallpaper* Group
Editor-in-Chief
Tony Chambers

Publishing Director
Andrew Black

Publisher
Neil Sumner

Contributors
Meirion Pritchard
Ellie Stathaki

Wallpaper* ® is a
registered trademark
of IPC Media Limited

All prices are correct at
time of going to press,
but are subject to change.

PHAIDON

Phaidon Press Limited
Regent's Wharf
All Saints Street
London N1 9PA

Phaidon Press Inc
180 Varick Street
New York, NY 10014

Phaidon® is a registered
trademark of Phaidon
Press Limited

www.phaidon.com

First published 2007
© 2007 IPC Media Limited

ISBN 978 0 7148 4738 2

A CIP Catalogue record for
this book is available from
the British Library.

Printed in China

PHOTOGRAPHERS

CHICAGO

A COLOUR-CODED GUIDE TO THE HOT 'HOODS

THE LOOP
An architects' playground, site of the world's first – and some of its finest – skyscrapers

LINCOLN PARK
Chicago's gilded youth have made this area their own, although its light is now fading

SOUTH LOOP
Capone-era warehouses loom over a renascent district of bars, bookshops and eateries

NEAR NORTH
The Magnificent Mile has to be the first port of call for any self-respecting retail junkie

WEST LOOP
From meatpackers to media packs, the former industrial zone is now an arty hangout

GOLD COAST
Extravagant residential architecture marks the home of the Windy City's wealthiest

LAKE VIEW
A blend of neighbourhoods, including sporty Wrigleyville and gay village Boystown

WICKER PARK
Picturesque townhouses and laid-back cafés attract a cool crowd of music and art types

For a full description of each neighbourhood, see the Introduction.
Featured venues are colour-coded, according to the district in which they are located.